SUMMER FOOD

PAUL LØWE

PHOTOGRAPHY BY NINA DREYER HENSLEY & JIM HENSLEY

SUM MER FOOD

NEW SUMMER CLASSICS

TRANSLATED BY SCOTT GIVOT, CCP

weldon**owen**

Copyright © Gyldendal Norsk Forlag AS 2013, Gyldendal Litteratur

Originally published as: SOMMERMAT

Weldon Owen, Inc. is a division of Bonnier Corporation

415 Jackson Street, Suite 200, San Francisco, CA 94111

Original cover design and layout by Kristine Lillevik

Translated by Scott Givot, CCP

Library of Congress Cataloging-in-Publication
data is available
ISBN 13: 978-1-61628-823-5
ISBN 10: 1-61628-823-X

www.weldonowen.com

Printed and bound in Latvia by Livonia Print SIA

This edition printed in 2014

10 9 8 7 6 5 4 3 2 1

SUMMER MEMORIES

Summer food is really all about memories for me. They are memories of long days at the cottage in Norway with Dad's barbeque, Mom's potato salad, glorious sunlight, and warm weather. It is also the memory of when we made this book, the first book collaboration of the triumvirate, Nina Dreyer, Jim Hensley, and me, Paul Løwe. We decided early on that we would photograph the whole book outside (in spite of Nina's phobia for mosquitoes and other insects and the fact that I believed that nature was overrated and would have preferred to stay in the city). The summer was characterized by masses of fresh air, outdoor toilets, food preparation in the tiniest cabin kitchens you can possibly imagine, and long evenings with a glass of wine. I wouldn't have traded that summer for anything. We wish you all a fantastic summer, whether it is in frigid January or during a beautiful sunset in August.

Paul Løwe

JUN
JUL
AUG

CHAPTER 1

BREAKFAST

It was Friday evening and I drove from the city with my girlfriend, Alex. We were on the way to her family's summer home, which was situated on a small island. It rained and the wind blustered, and I was preoccupied with the notion that we must ride in a small boat in order to get to the cottage. I can't exactly call myself the king of the sea . . . and I was right. When we arrived at the boat, which was considerably smaller than Alex had described, the rain blew sideways. We crossed over all the same, and I was drenched from head to toe. Not only was I wet, but sour as a lemon (I don't like being wet). So, I went to bed and slept through to the next day, when I awoke to the sound of the water and seagulls in the distance. The sunlight poured into the room and with that all apprehension dissipated from my shoulders. I stood up and slinked away like a coward. There was Alex's mom, Pia, standing at the entry with freshly baked rolls, the coffee was prepared, and we sat around the table outside and chatted about how unseaworthy Løwe was. Thirty minutes later we set the breakfast table along the water's edge. We ate and drank with much laughter and conversation. This was years ago, and I can still recall it as though it was yesterday. The morale was tops and a good breakfast (and a beach) added to the enjoyment of life.

EGGS BENEDICT À LA NORWAY

4 servings

1 teaspoon vinegar

4 large eggs

3¼ oz (100 g) baby spinach

4 slices toast

8 slices smoked salmon

salt and freshly cracked pepper

Bring a large pot of water to a simmer. Add the vinegar. Break 1 egg at a time over the water and carefully let it drop into the pot. Let the eggs simmer for 2 minutes. Remove the eggs with a slotted spoon and set them to dry on a paper towel. Meanwhile, pour about 1 inch of water into a saucepan and bring to a boil. Place a steamer over the boiling water, add the spinach to the steamer, cover the pan, and steam until wilted, 1–2 minutes. On each slice of toast, layer a small amount of the steamed spinach, 2 slices of smoked salmon, and 1 egg, sprinkle with salt and pepper, and serve.

VARIATION
You can also use another type of smoked fish, such as smoked trout or mackerel.

RICOTTA PANCAKES WITH PLUMS

4 servings

1½ cups (6 oz/185 g) all-purpose flour

1 teaspoon baking powder

½ cup (4 oz/126 g) sugar

4 large eggs, yolks and whites separated

1¼ cups (12 fl oz/375 ml) whole milk

1 cup (8 oz/250 g) ricotta cheese

butter, for frying

6 plums, pitted and sliced

pure maple syrup, for serving

Mix together the flour, baking powder, sugar, egg yolks, milk, and ricotta in a large bowl. Whisk the egg whites separately in a small bowl and carefully fold them into the flour mixture. Place the batter in the refrigerator for 15 minutes. When ready to cook the pancakes, warm some butter (about 2 teaspoons per pancake) in a frying pan over medium heat. Ladle in some batter and lay plum slices over the surface. Cook for about 2 minutes, then flip and cook for 2 more minutes, until golden. Serve the pancakes with syrup.

VARIATIONS

You can substitute other fruits like apricots, bananas, or apples in place of the plums. Nuts may also be used.

THESE ARE CLASSIC PANCAKES WITH
A LITTLE TWIST. YOU'LL LOVE THIS RECIPE.

A FRITTATA IS A CROSS BETWEEN AN OMELET AND A PIE. SUPER EASY TO MAKE, IT'S THE PERFECT DISH TO SERVE FOLLOWING A MORNING WALK.

FRITTATA WITH THREE CHEESES & GREEN ONION

4 servings

1 teaspoon olive oil

3 green onions, thinly sliced

8 large eggs

6 tablespoons heavy cream

3 tablespoons ricotta cheese

2 tablespoons grated parmesan

3 tablespoons grated jarlsberg or emmentaler cheese

½ teaspoon salt

¼ teaspoon freshly cracked pepper

4 fresh sprigs thyme, finely chopped

Preheat the oven to 350°F (180°C). Heat the oil in a nonstick pan and sauté the onions until soft. Mix together the eggs, cream, cheeses, salt, and pepper in a medium bowl. Pour the egg mixture into the pan with the onions and sprinkle the thyme over the top. Cook for 10–12 minutes, or until the bottom of the frittata is golden brown. Serve warm or at room temperature.

SERVING TIP
This dish tastes great served with bread and slices of prosciutto or ham.

BREAKFAST PIZZA

4 servings (4 small pizzas)

2 teaspoons yeast

2 cups (16 fl oz/500 ml) warm water

1 tablespoon honey

½ cup (2½ oz/75 g) all-purpose flour

3 tablespoons olive oil, plus 4 teaspoons

2 teaspoons salt

3½ oz (105 g) baby spinach

2–3 oz thinly sliced pancetta, cut in strips

flaked sea salt, for sprinkling

freshly cracked pepper, for sprinkling

4 large eggs

Mix together the yeast, water, and honey in a mixing bowl and let stand for 5 minutes. Add the flour, a little at a time, stirring to combine. Add the 3 tablespoons oil and the salt and knead the dough well. Cover the bowl with plastic wrap and leave the dough to rise for approximately 2 hours.

Preheat the oven to 425°F (220°C). Roll the dough and divide into 4 equal parts. Press or roll out each ball of dough into a small pizza. Transfer the pizzas to a sheet pan lined with parchment paper. Spread the spinach and pancetta over the top of each pizza, dividing it evenly, drizzle with the remaining 4 teaspoons oil, and sprinkle with some sea salt and pepper. Bake for 6–8 minutes. Remove the pan from the oven and gently crack an egg over the middle of each pizza. Continue to bake until the eggs are firm, about another 4 minutes.

WHO SAYS THAT PIZZA IS ONLY FOR LUNCH OR SUPPER? I SERVE THIS FOR BRUNCH, AND IT'S ALWAYS A HUGE HIT!

EGGS AND SMOKED SALMON BELONG TOGETHER. THIS IS AN UNBELIEVABLY SIMPLE BREAKFAST AND IT DOESN'T REQUIRE MUCH CLEANING UP EITHER.

BAKED EGGS WITH SMOKED SALMON

4 servings

butter, for greasing

8 large eggs

8 slices smoked salmon, cut into thin strips

¾ cup (6 fl oz/180 ml) heavy cream

salt and freshly cracked pepper

fresh dill, snipped into small pieces, for garnish

toasted bread, for serving

Preheat the oven to 325°F (165°C). Grease 4 small ramekins or ovenproof baking cups with butter. Crack 2 eggs into each ramekin. Divide the smoked salmon evenly among the ramekins and top with equal portions of the cream and salt and pepper to taste. Gently stir the contents of each ramekin, being careful not to break the yolks. Bake the eggs for 12–15 minutes, or until the egg has firmed. Top the ramekins with dill pieces, and serve hot with toasted bread.

BAKED FRENCH TOAST WITH AMARETTO & CHERRIES

4 servings

3 large eggs

1 cup (8 fl oz/250 ml) whole milk

3 tablespoons sugar

1 teaspoon vanilla sugar

2 tablespoons amaretto

1 loaf brioche or soft white bread, sliced

1 cup (6 oz/185 g) cherries, pitted

pure maple syrup, for serving

Preheat the oven to 350°F (180°C). Whisk together the eggs, milk, sugar, vanilla sugar, and Amaretto in a large mixing bowl. Place the bread slices in a nonstick ovenproof pan and pour the egg mixture over the top. Allow the bread to absorb the egg mixture for about 15 minutes. Scatter the cherries over the top, then bake for 15–20 minutes, until golden brown. Serve warm with maple syrup.

COOKING TIP

You can prepare this dish the evening before, cover and refrigerate, then bake the French toast in the morning.

AMARETTO GIVES FRENCH TOAST
A LITTLE ADDITIONAL FLAVOR
AND THE AROMA OF ALMONDS.
INCREDIBLY GOOD!

MAKING ONE'S OWN BREAKFAST
CEREAL IS FUN AND YOU GET TO USE
JUST THE INGREDIENTS YOU LIKE BEST.

PAUL'S BREAKFAST CEREAL

20 servings

2 cups (12 oz/370 g) rolled oat flakes

½ cup (3 oz/90 g) pumpkin seeds

¼ cup (2 oz/60 g) hazelnuts

¼ cup (2 oz/60 g) cashews

4 tablespoons (3 oz/90 g) honey

½ cup (3 oz/90 g) dried cranberries

½ cup (3 oz/90 g) dried mango

½ cup (3 oz/90 g) dried goji berries

Preheat the oven to 350°F (180°C). Thoroughly mix the oats, pumpkin seeds, hazelnuts, cashews, and honey together in a mixing bowl and pour onto a baking sheet. Roast until the mixture starts to brown, about 15 minutes. Remove from the oven and let cool. Transfer the cereal to a sealed container. Add the dried cranberries, mango, and goji berries and blend with your hands. The cereal will keep for up to 2 weeks.

I'VE USED ASPARAGUS HERE,
BUT YOU CAN CERTAINLY USE
ANOTHER TYPE OF VEGETABLE.

BREAKFAST TORTILLA

4 servings

16 spears asparagus, trimmed (see tip)

1 tablespoon butter

8 eggs

8 tablespoons (4 fl oz/120 ml) heavy cream

salt and freshly cracked pepper

4 medium tortillas, white flour or corn

1 small red onion, finely chopped

¼ teaspoon red pepper flakes

4 sprigs fresh dill

4 lime wedges

Bring a pot of salted water to a boil and cook the asparagus for 1 minute. Transfer the asparagus to a bowl filled with cold water. Meanwhile, heat the butter in a nonstick skillet over medium heat. Break the eggs into a bowl, add the cream and a pinch each of salt and pepper, and whisk until well blended. Add the eggs to the skillet and cook, stirring with a spatula, until soft curds form, 5–8 minutes. Place 4 asparagus spears in the center of each tortilla and divide the scrambled eggs on top. Sprinkle the onion and red pepper flakes over the top. Garnish with a sprig of dill and serve with a lime wedge.

COOKING TIP

To trim asparagus, hold the spear with one hand on each end, and bend it in two. The breaking point will be where the division between the tender part and the hard stalk is located. Use the hard stalk for stock or discard.

FRESH STRAWBERRY JAM

1 large container, or about 2 lb (32 oz/1 kg)

2 lb (32 oz/1 kg) strawberries, rinsed and stems removed

3½ oz (105 g) sugar

2 teaspoons lemon juice

There are many ways to make a simple fresh jam, but I place the strawberries, sugar, and lemon juice in a bowl and mash them with a big fork. Mash the mixture until it is a suitable jam-like consistency. Add the jam to a glass jar and cover with an airtight top.

VARIATIONS

You can try this same method with raspberries, blueberries, red currants, or gooseberries.

YOGURT WITH CHERRY COMPOTE

4 servings

6½ oz (200 g) cherries, pitted

1½ oz (45 g) sugar

2 teaspoons lemon juice

2 cups (16 oz/500 g) plain yogurt

seeds from ½ vanilla pod

Combine the cherries, sugar, and lemon juice in a saucepan, cover, and cook over medium heat until the mixture thickens, about 12 minutes. Remove the mixture from the heat. Combine the yogurt and vanilla seeds in a small bowl and divide the mixture into 4 glasses or bowls. Top each serving with the warm cherry compote and serve.

SERVING TIP
This compote also tastes good with grilled chicken.

CHAPTER 2

LUNCH

I have always loved water. I love to bathe both in the sea and the bathtub. But as much as I love it, I am not much of a seaman. I have often imagined that if I had been on board the Titanic, I would have been the first to drown.

My family had a cottage in Norway and with the house came an old wooden boat, which we named the SS Beauty. Dad loved to putter and polish the boat all through the winter, but I could never appreciate his fascination with those activities. I remember one summer day when the whole family woke up early, packed a big basket of sandwiches, and set our course toward a slope of bare rock in the sea. We carried on there the whole day, eating, drinking and making ourselves cozy. On the way back to the mainland, my dad said to me, "Paul, now perhaps you understand why I love this boat and spend so much time with it." "Yep, dad, I understand!"

GRILLED POTATO SALAD WITH LEMON & PARSLEY

4 servings

1 lb (16 oz/500 g) small potatoes, halved

6 baby red onions, sliced lengthwise

4 green onions, whiteish-green parts only, trimmed

2 cups (16 fl oz/500 ml) olive oil

salt and freshly cracked pepper

zest and juice from 1 lemon

3 teaspoons finely chopped flat-leaf parsley

1 teaspoon capers, chopped

Combine the potatoes, baby red onions, green onions, 1 cup (8 fl oz/250 ml) oil, and salt and pepper to taste in a bowl and mix well. Place the potatoes and onions in the middle of a hot grill and grill until brown and tender, 10–12 minutes. High heat on a gas grill is best for this. Transfer the grilled vegetables to a bowl and add the lemon zest and juice, the remaining 1 cup (8 fl oz/250 ml) oil, parsley, and capers. Add salt and pepper to taste. Mix well and serve.

THIS SALAD IS TERRIFIC! WHEN THE POTATOES SOAK UP ALL THE ACIDIC DRESSING, EACH BITE IS DELICIOUS.

HEIRLOOM TOMATO & MOZZARELLA SALAD

4 servings

1½ lb (24 oz/750 g) baby heirloom tomatoes, halved

6½ oz (200 g) mozzarella cheese, torn into small pieces

1 bunch fresh basil, leaves only

olive oil, for dressing

salt and freshly cracked pepper

Spread out the tomatoes on a large plate or serving platter. Add the mozzarella and basil on top of the tomatoes, then cover with as much oil as desired. Season with salt and pepper.

SERVING TIP
Serve this salad with grilled fresh tuna, chicken, or sliced sirloin steak for a summer dinner.

> SUMMER IS THE BEST TIME OF YEAR FOR TOMATOES, WHICH MEANS IT IS ACTUALLY THE ONLY TIME OF YEAR WHEN I EAT THEM. TRY TO FIND THE BEST SELECTION OF HEIRLOOM TOMATOES AVAILABLE FOR THIS SIMPLE SALAD.

ASIAN CUCUMBER SALAD

4 servings

1 english cucumber, halved lengthwise and thinly sliced

½ red onion, thinly sliced

1 teaspoon grated lemon zest

¼ teaspoon red pepper flakes

1 teaspoon finely chopped fresh dill

3 tablespoons rice vinegar

1 tablespoon lemon juice

1 teaspoon sugar

Combine the cucumber, red onion, lemon zest, red pepper flakes, and dill in a bowl. Whisk together the vinegar, lemon juice, and sugar and pour over the salad and toss gently. For the best flavor, let the salad stand for 1 hour before serving.

SERVING TIP

For a fancier presentation, score the cucumber skin with a citrus zester before slicing.

MY VARIATION OF THIS CLASSIC CUCUMBER SALAD IS NO BETTER THAN THE TRADITIONAL STYLE BUT IT HAS A LITTLE MORE KICK.

MY MOM MADE THIS INCREDIBLY SIMPLE
POTATO SALAD EVERY SUMMER, AND
IT BRINGS BACK MANY GOOD MEMORIES.

MOM'S POTATO SALAD

4 servings

1 lb (16 oz/500 g) small new potatoes

3 cups (24 oz/750 g) light sour cream

½ cup (4 fl oz/125 g) mayonnaise

2 teaspoons sweet mustard

salt and freshly cracked pepper

1 small red onion, finely chopped

2 teaspoons finely chopped chives

Bring a pot of salted water to a boil over medium heat and cook the potatoes until tender. Drain the potatoes, then peel and slice them into thin pieces. Place the potato slices in a bowl. In another bowl, mix together the sour cream, mayonnaise, mustard, and salt and pepper to taste. Fold the potatoes into the sour cream mixture. Add the red onion and chives and mix well. Refrigerate the salad for 1 hour before serving.

VARIATIONS
If you want a potato salad with a little more kick, substitute dijon or another strong-flavored mustard for the sweet mustard.

GRILLED PIZZA

4 servings (4 pizzas)

2 teaspoons yeast	½ cup (2½ oz/77 g) roasted pine nuts
2 cups (16 fl oz/500 ml) warm water	1 bunch fresh basil,
1 teaspoon honey	plus leaves to garnish
½ cup (2½ oz/75 g) all-purpose flour	1 clove garlic, finely chopped
9 tablespoons (4 fl oz/130 ml)	1 cup (4 oz/125 g) grated parmesan
olive oil, plus more for greasing	12 slices prosciutto
salt and freshly cracked pepper	

Combine the yeast, water, and honey in a mixing bowl. Let the mixture stand for 5 minutes. Add the flour, a little at a time, stirring continuously. Add 3 tablespoons oil and ½ teaspoon salt and knead the dough well. Cover the bowl with plastic wrap and let the dough rise in a warm place. Make the pesto. Chop the pine nuts and basil and place in a bowl. Add the garlic and Parmesan and mix. Add the remaining 6 tablespoons (3 fl oz/90 ml) oil. If the sauce is too dry, add a little more oil. Add salt and pepper to taste.

Knead the dough and divide into 4 equal parts. Press or roll out each part into a small pizza. Lay each pizza on a piece of baking paper that is greased with oil. Brush the surface with oil. Turn the paper quickly over a hot grill, so that only the pizza crust lies flat on the grill. Grill the crust for 2–3 minutes, turn, and cook further on the other side. Take the pizza crust off the grill and add the pesto, prosciutto, and basil leaves. Serve at once.

COOKING TIP
You can use the topping of your choice on the pizza, but since it takes only a few short moments to grill, you don't get a regular cheese pizza.

YES, YOU CAN MAKE PIZZA ON THE GRILL.
IT'S ACTUALLY VERY SIMPLE AND THE
CRUST BECOMES FANTASTICALLY CRISPY.

I LOVE THE BLEND OF TOMATOES AND
THYME AND WONDERED, HOW WOULD
IT WORK AS A TART? HEAVENLY.

TOMATO & THYME TART

4 servings

2 puff pastry sheets

all-purpose flour, for sprinkling

40 cherry tomatoes, halved

fresh thyme, snipped into small pieces, for garnish

salt and freshly cracked pepper

2 tablespoons olive oil

Preheat the oven to 425°F (220°C). Divide each sheet of puff pastry in half and press or roll it out to double the size. Sprinkle a little flour on the kitchen counter under the pastry sheet to avoid sticking of the dough. Lay the puff pastry on a sheet pan covered with baking paper. Use a sharp knife and cut a small incision around the border of the dough, roughly ⅜ inch (1 cm). Cover the surface with the tomatoes, thyme, and season with salt and pepper. Drizzle the oil over the top. Bake until golden brown, approximately 12 minutes.

VARIATIONS
Lay some slices of mozzarella over the top of the tart for a delicious caprese.

AVOCADO TOAST WITH LEMON & CHILE

4 servings

2 ripe avocadoes

2 slices of toasted rustic country bread

flaked sea salt, for sprinkling

red pepper flakes, for sprinkling

1 teaspoon grated lemon zest

juice of 1 lemon

olive oil, for drizzling

Divide the avocado in half, remove the pit and carefully remove the skin. Slice the avocado into thin boats. Divide the toast on a plate and spread the avocado, salt, red pepper flakes, lemon zest, lemon juice, and drizzle a little oil over the top. Ready to serve!

SERVING TIP
Add some slices of grilled chicken or tuna, if you desire a more substantial meal.

THIS IS ONE OF MY FAVORITE SNACKS.
IT'S SIMPLE AND VERY TASTY.

ALL FLAVORS HERE ARE IN PERFECT
HARMONY: SWEET APRICOTS,
SALTY CURED HAM, AND ACIDIC CHEESE.

BAKED APRICOTS WITH CURED HAM & GOAT CHEESE

4 servings

½ lb (8 oz/250 g) fresh apricots, halved

4 tablespoons (2 fl oz/60 ml) olive oil, plus 2 teaspoons

8 oz (250 g) mixed salad greens

12 thin slices cured ham, chopped in small bits

1 cup (5 oz/155 g) goat cheese, crumbled

1 small red onion, sliced in thin rings

salt and freshly cracked pepper

1 teaspoon lemon juice

Preheat the oven to 350°F (180°C). Spread the apricots on a nonstick sheet pan and splash with the 2 teaspoons oil. Bake until the apricots cook through, approximately 7 minutes. Divide the greens between 4 plates and place the apricots, ham, goat cheese, and onion over the top. Sprinkle a little salt and pepper over the top. Whisk the 4 tablespoons (2 fl oz/60 ml) oil and lemon juice together and pour over the salad.

COOKING TIP

I've always used very little salt and pepper on the salads that I prepare. Try tasting them with and without, and you will soon realize that salads without seasoning and herbs taste rather dreary.

GRILLED CORN SALAD

4 servings

4 ears of corn, shucked and washed

olive oil, for coating

salt and freshly cracked pepper

¼ teaspoon of red pepper flakes

24 cherry tomatoes, halved

1 small red onion, thinly sliced

fresh basil leaves, for garnish

fresh thyme, for garnish

Start by rubbing the ears of corn with oil, salt, pepper, and the red pepper flakes. Lay them in the center of a hot grill and brown them until they are colored on all sides. Transfer the corn to a cutting board and, once they have cooled, use a sharp knife to slice the corn away from the cobs. Lay the corn in a bowl and toss with the tomatoes, onion, and some basil and thyme. Dress the salad with a little oil and season with salt and pepper.

COOKING TIP

Many recipes state that you should cook the corn a few minutes before placing the cobs on the grill. You can do this, but you lose some of the fantastic crunchiness that fresh corn has. I think this method is a little sad, so I never cook the corn before grilling.

THINGS REALLY COME ALIVE ON THE GRILL. CORN, IN PARTICULAR, RENDERS A MARVELOUS SWEET TASTE FROM THE HEAT. THIS IS A VERY SIMPLE, GOOD, AND FAST SUMMER SALAD TO MAKE.

GRILLED SPRING CABBAGE WITH PLUMS & GOAT CHEESE

4 servings

10 plums, halved

olive oil, for coating

10 oz (315 g) spring cabbage, or napa variety, leaves separated and washed

1 cup (5 oz/155 g) goat cheese, crumbled

handful of fresh basil leaves

salt and freshly cracked pepper

Coat the plums with a little oil. Place them in the center of a hot grill and cook them for approximately 1½ minutes on each side. Transfer the plums to a platter. Place the cabbage leaves on the grill and brown rapidly on each side. Once there is good color, remove them from the grill and transfer them to the platter. You can tear them up into smaller pieces, but I prefer the whole leaves. Add the cheese, the basil, and sprinkle with salt and pepper to taste. Finish the salad with a little oil.

SPRING CABBAGE IS CONSUMED FAR TOO LITTLE IN OUR DIET. THE TASTE IS FANTASTIC AND IT IS HEALTHIER TO EAT THAN SPINACH. JUST A FEW SECONDS ON THE GRILL RENDERS A SMOKY, DELICIOUS TASTE.

CABBAGE CAESAR SALAD WITH AIOLI

4 servings

1 egg yolk	2 slices of rustic country bread
pinch of maldon or flaked sea salt	olive oil, for brushing
¼ teaspoon freshly cracked pepper	6½ oz (200 g) spring or napa
¼ teaspoon powdered mustard	cabbage, shredded
¾ cup (6 fl oz/180 ml) corn oil	1½ oz (45 g) grated parmesan
1 tablespoon lemon juice	fresh thyme sprigs, for garnish

Begin with the aioli. Whisk the egg yolk in a bowl and add the salt, pepper, and powdered mustard. Pour the corn oil in a thin stream into the bowl and continue to whisk vigorously until the sauce turns shiny. Add the lemon juice and taste to determine if you need more salt. Brush both sides of the sliced bread with a little olive oil and toast on both sides until a golden brown color is visible. Cut the bread in thin strips. Divide the cabbage, croutons, and Parmesan between 4 plates and garnish with some thyme. Pour the aioli over the top and serve.

SERVING TIP

This aioli can have many uses: as a dip or condiment to grilled chicken, fish, vegetables, sandwiches, and so much more.

THIS IS MY VARIATION OF A CAESAR SALAD. I USE CABBAGE AS AN ALTERNATIVE TO ROMAINE GREENS. IT'S INCREDIBLY GOOD AND HEALTHY.

THIS DISH IS FANTASTIC
AS AN ACCOMPANIMENT
TO CHICKEN OR FISH.

GRILLED CARROTS WITH HONEY & DILL

4 servings

1 lb (16 oz/500 g) carrots

3 tablespoons honey

1 teaspoon fresh dill, chopped

¼ teaspoon salt

Peel the carrots, but leave a little of the green stalk at the top. Place the carrots in the center of a hot grill and brown thoroughly on all sides. Transfer the carrots to a platter, drizzle with the honey and sprinkle the dill and salt on top. Serve this dish warm.

VARIATIONS

Other vegetables are also complimented in taste by honey, like beets, fennel, parsley root, and rutabaga.

ORZO SALAD WITH GRILLED CORN, OLIVES & BASIL

4 servings

2 ears of corn	DRESSING
olive oil, for coating	4 tablespoons (2 fl oz/60 ml) olive oil
salt and freshly cracked pepper	4 teaspoons lemon juice
20 cherry tomatoes, halved	1 teaspoon powdered mustard
½ red onion, finely chopped	¼ teaspoon each salt, freshly cracked
2 oz (60 g) pitted kalamata	pepper, and red pepper flakes
or black olives	
½ bunch fresh basil, leaves only	
½ lb (8 oz/250 g) orzo pasta,	
cooked al dente	

Rub the ears of corn with oil, salt, pepper, and red pepper flakes. Transfer them to the center of a hot grill and brown them until there is color over the entire surface. On a cutting board, use a sharp knife to slice the corn away from the cobs. Combine the corn in a bowl along with the tomatoes, red onion, olives, basil, and orzo. Whisk the dressing ingredients together and pour over the salad. Mix well and serve.

SERVING TIP

Grilled shrimp taste great as an accompaniment in this salad.

ORZO IS A RICE-SHAPED PASTA THAT CAN BE SUBSTITUTED WITH COOKED COUSCOUS OR BULGUR WHEAT.

SEAFOOD SALAD

4 servings

6½ oz (200 g) fresh crabmeat or crayfish, cut in small pieces

6½ oz (200 g) fresh or frozen baby shrimp

1 teaspoon lemon zest, finely chopped

2 tablespoons lemon juice

5 tablespoons mayonnaise

2 tablespoons leeks, sliced finely in thin strips

1 teaspoon caviar, small red eggs (optional)

2 tablespoons fresh dill, finely chopped

salt and freshly cracked pepper

Mix together the crabmeat, shrimp, lemon zest, lemon juice, mayonnaise, leeks, caviar, and dill in a bowl. Season the salad with salt and pepper to taste.

SERVING TIP
Serve with toast or fill the cavity of an avocado half with this seafood salad.

MUSSEL SOUP

4 servings

½ cup dry white wine

2 lb (32 oz/1 kg) mussels, rinsed and cleaned

2 tablespoons butter

2 shallots, finely chopped

2 cloves garlic, finely chopped

1 tablespoon all-purpose flour

4 cups (32 fl oz/1 l) fish stock

1½ cups (12 fl oz/ 375 ml) heavy (double) cream

salt and freshly cracked pepper

2 tablespoons fresh dill, finely chopped

Combine the wine and mussels in a large pot and set over high heat on the stovetop. Steam the mussels with the lid on the pot for 3–4 minutes, or until the shells open. Discard any mussels that have not opened. Strain the liquid from the pot and reserve in a bowl. Remove the cooked mussels from the shells and transfer the mussels to a bowl. Wipe the pot clean. Transfer the pot back to the stovetop and set on medium heat. Melt the butter in the pot and sauté the shallots and garlic until soft and translucent. Whisk in the flour until absorbed in the mixture, add the fish stock and reserved mussel liquid, and continue to whisk vigorously to avoid clumps forming. Lower the heat and simmer for 10 minutes. Whisk in the cream, salt and pepper to taste, and the dill and simmer for an additional 10 minutes. Ladle the soup into shallow bowls, garnishing with the cooked mussels.

MY MOTHER'S RECIPE IS PERFECT EVERY TIME. SHE ALSO ADDS PEELED BABY SHRIMP TO THE SOUP.

THIS IS A GOOD OLD CLASSIC
THAT HAS FOLLOWED ME THROUGH
THE YEARS AND IS ALWAYS TASTY.

ASPARAGUS & RICOTTA TART

4 servings

1¼ cups (6½ oz/200 g) all-purpose flour	1 cup (8 oz/250 g) ricotta cheese
salt and freshly cracked pepper	6 tablespoons (2 fl oz/60 ml) heavy (double) cream
6 tablespoons (3 oz/90 g) cold unsalted butter, cut in small bits	6 tablespoons (2 fl oz/60 ml) whole milk
3–4 tablespoons cold water	1 lb (16 oz/500 g) asparagus
1 large egg	

Combine the flour, 1 teaspoon salt, and ¼ teaspoon pepper in a bowl. Add the butter and work it into the flour with your fingers. The result will be a grainy mixture. Add the water and work it into the dough quickly until thoroughly combined. Cover the bowl with plastic wrap and leave in the refrigerator for at least one hour before use. Transfer the dough into a buttered nonstick pie pan, about 8½ inches (21.5 cm) in circumference, smooth, and press out to the edges. Transfer the pan to the freezer for at least 15 minutes before pre-baking the pie shell. Bake the shell at 400°F (200°C) for approximately 10 minutes, or until the dough becomes a pale golden color. Remove the crust from the oven. Mix the egg, cheese, cream, milk, and salt and pepper to taste together and spoon the mixture into the tart shell. Cut down the length of each asparagus spear and lay each piece in the pie in an attractive pattern. Bake the pie at 350°F (180°C) for approximately 20 minutes or until the filling is firm and the crust is brown. Serve the tart either hot or at room temperature.

CORN & POTATO SOUP WITH SMOKED FISH

4 servings

2 tablespoons butter

1 medium onion, finely chopped

1 celery stalk, finely chopped

4 cups (32 fl oz/1 l) chicken stock

12 small new potatoes, halved

corn kernels from 3 ears of corn

1 cup (8 fl oz/250 ml) heavy cream

2 tablespoons fresh dill, coarsely chopped

salt and freshly cracked pepper

⅓ lb (5 oz/155 g) boneless smoked trout, mackerel, or salmon

Melt the butter in a pot and sauté the onion and celery until tender. Add the stock and potatoes and bring to a boil. Let the soup simmer for 10 minutes. Add the corn, cream, and dill to the soup and simmer for an additional 10 minutes. Add salt and pepper to taste. Cut the fish into bite-sized pieces and divide into 4 portions and serve as a garnish with the hot soup.

SERVING TIP

You can serve this soup without the fish, and as an alternative it tastes delicious with crispy bacon bits or cooked shrimp.

THIS SOUP HAS THE TASTE OF SUMMER.

QUINOA IS FABULOUS IN SALADS.
IT HAS A LIGHT AND FLUFFY TEXTURE
AND ABSORBS DRESSING WELL.

QUINOA SALAD WITH TOMATOES & CAPER DRESSING

4 servings

zest from 1 lemon, finely chopped

2 tablespoons lemon juice

4 tablespoons (2 fl oz/60 ml) olive oil

1 teaspoon honey

1 tablespoon capers

¼ teaspoon red pepper flakes

salt and freshly cracked pepper

10 oz (315 g) quinoa, cooked and cooled at room temperature

24 cherry tomatoes, halved

1 small bunch of fresh basil, leaves only

Combine the lemon zest, lemon juice, oil, honey, capers, red pepper flakes, and salt and pepper to taste together and whisk vigorously. Add the quinoa to a bowl and add the tomatoes, basil, and dressing and mix thoroughly.

VARIATIONS

Here again you can add other vegetables if you desire, or fish, chicken, or seafood in bite-sized pieces.

PURE AND SIMPLE LOBSTER SALAD
SERVED ON A BUTTERED AND
BROWNED HOT DOG BUN IS HEAVENLY.

LOBSTER ROLLS

4 servings

1 cooked lobster

2 tablespoons chives, finely chopped

1 teaspoon lemon zest, finely chopped

juice from ½ lemon

½ cup (4 fl oz/125 ml) mayonnaise

1 tablespoon sour cream

salt and freshly cracked pepper

1 tablespoon butter

4 hot dog buns

Remove all the lobster meat from the shell and chop it into small bits. Mix the lobster meat with the chives, lemon zest, lemon juice, mayonnaise, sour cream, and salt and pepper to taste in a bowl. Heat the butter in a large pan and fry the buns to a golden brown on each side. Serve the lobster salad in the hot dog buns.

VARIATION

If you think lobster meat is too rich, you can substitute it with fresh baby shrimp. Next to just as good!

TROUT SALAD WITH POTATOES & LEMON SOUR CREAM

4 servings

20 small new potatoes, halved	**DRESSING**
1 fresh trout fillet	¾ cup (6 fl oz/180 ml) light
salt and freshly cracked pepper	sour cream
2 tablespoons olive oil	1 tablespoon lemon zest,
1½ English cucumbers	finely chopped
1 small head butter lettuce,	2 tablespoons lemon juice
leaves separated	1 tablespoon fresh dill,
1 small red onion, finely sliced	finely chopped
1 tablespoon capers	1 tablespoon mustard powder
small handful fresh dill,	
coarsely chopped	

Place the potatoes and trout in a nonstick pan and sprinkle with salt and pepper. Coat the mixture with the oil and roast at 350°F (180°C). Remove the fish after 10 minutes and continue roasting the potatoes until tender. Allow the potatoes to cool to room temperature. Halve the cucumbers, then thinly slice. Divide the fish into bite-sized bits and gently toss together with the lettuce, potatoes, red onion, cucumber, capers, and dill. Mix together the sour cream, lemon zest, lemon juice, dill, mustard powder, and salt and pepper to taste in a separate bowl. Serve the salad with the dressing on the side.

SERVING TIP
Use this dressing as a dip for raw vegetables or chips.

THIS IS A TRULY GOOD SOUP IN WHICH
I USE BOTH DRIED MUSHROOMS
AND FRESH CHANTERELLES.

CREAMED MUSHROOM & PANCETTA SOUP

4 servings

3 cups (3 oz/90 g) dried shiitake mushrooms, sliced

½ cup (½ oz/90 g) dried porcini mushrooms, sliced

2 cups (16 fl oz/500 mg) boiling water

1 tablespoon butter

1 tablespoon olive oil

1 small red onion, finely chopped

2 cloves garlic, finely chopped

3½ oz (105 g) pancetta or bacon, sliced and cut in small pieces

10 oz (305 g) fresh wild mushroom assortment, brushed, thinly sliced

2 cups (16 fl oz/500 mg) chicken stock

½ cup (4 fl oz/125 ml) heavy (double) cream

salt and freshly cracked pepper

Set the dried mushrooms in a bowl and pour the boiling water over the top. Leave the mushrooms to stand in the water for 10 minutes and cover the bowl with a plate. Strain the mushrooms after a few minutes and reserve the soaking water and mushrooms separately. Heat the butter and oil in a large pan and sauté the onion, garlic, and pancetta until the meat browns. Add the reconstituted and fresh mushrooms to the pan. Sauté the mushrooms for 5 minutes, then remove a few of them in order to garnish the top of each serving. Pour the chicken stock and the reserved mushroom water into the pan. Let the soup simmer for 25 minutes. Pour the soup into a blender and blend on high until it becomes a smooth purée. Pour the soup back into the pan and whisk in the cream. Bring the soup to a boil and add salt and pepper to taste. Ladle the soup into 4 bowls, decorating with a few sliced mushrooms on top as garnish.

PASTA WITH POACHED EGG & ASPARAGUS

4 servings

1 lb (500 g) asparagus spears

½ lb (250 g) spaghetti, cooked al dente and drained

2 tablespoons white wine vinegar

4 large eggs

½ cup (2 oz/60 g) parmesan, sliced on a cheese plane

2 tablespoons chives, finely chopped

4 tablespoons (2 fl oz/60 ml) olive oil

salt and freshly cracked pepper

Boil a large pot of water and cook the asparagus for 30 seconds. Drain the asparagus and place equal portions of spaghetti and asparagus on 4 plates. Bring a large pot of water with the vinegar to a simmer. Break 1 egg at a time over the water and carefully let it drop into the pot. Let the eggs simmer for 2 minutes. Remove the eggs with a slotted spoon and place one egg over each plate of pasta. Sprinkle the Parmesan, chives, oil, and salt to taste over each serving of pasta. Crack the pepper over the top and serve.

THIS DISH MAKES A DELICIOUS LUNCH
AND THE POACHED EGG
BECOMES THE PASTA SAUCE.

THIS IS MY VARIATION OF A SALADE NIÇOISE.
I USE FRESH TUNA INSTEAD OF CANNED.
IF YOU CAN'T FIND FRESH FISH, THEN
USE THE CANNED VARIETY.

TUNA FISH SALAD

4 servings

10 oz (315 g) tuna fillet	8 radishes, halved
olive oil, for coating	fresh dill, broken into bits,
salt and freshly cracked pepper	for garnish
4 soft-cooked eggs, peeled	**DRESSING**
1 small head romaine lettuce,	4 tablespoons (2 fl oz/60 ml)
10 oz (315 g), cleaned and	olive oil
leaves broken	2 tablespoons mirin
½ english cucumber,	1 tablespoon shallot, finely chopped
sliced into strips	

Rub the tuna fillet with oil, salt, and pepper. Transfer the tuna to the center of a hot grill, and cook for approximately 2 minutes on each side. Slice the tuna into pieces ¾ inch (2 cm) thick. Cut the eggs in half. Divide the tuna, lettuce, cucumber, radishes, and egg halves evenly between 4 plates. Whisk together all the ingredients for the dressing, add salt and pepper to taste, and pour over the salads. Garnish with fresh dill.

SERVING TIP

If you use tuna from the can, choose one that is packed in water. I think this has the best taste.

GRILLED BEEF SALAD WITH TOMATO VINAIGRETTE

4 servings

1 large tomato, seeded and finely chopped	1 small head (½ lb/250 g) butter lettuce, leaves broken
1 shallot, finely chopped	14 cherry tomatoes, halved
2 tablespoons mirin	½ english cucumber, sliced in thin stalks
4 tablespoons (2 fl oz/60 ml) olive oil	fresh basil leaves, for garnish
1 teaspoon lime juice	fresh cilantro leaves, for garnish
¼ teaspoon red pepper flakes	1 lime, sliced in wedges
salt and freshly cracked pepper	
13 oz (410 g) sirloin steak	

Begin with the vinaigrette. Whisk together the tomato, shallot, mirin, oil, lime juice, and red pepper flakes in a mixing bowl. Add salt to taste. Rub the beef well with salt and pepper and transfer to the center of a hot grill, and cook for approximately 3 minutes on each side. Transfer the beef to a cutting board and wait at least 10 minutes before slicing it into pieces ¾ inch (2 cm) thick. Divide the lettuce, beef, tomatoes, and cucumber in equal portions and pour the vinaigrette over the top of each salad. Garnish with basil and cilantro. Serve with lime wedges on the side to squeeze extra juice over the top.

SERVING TIP

This vinaigrette tastes incredibly good with chicken and white fish.

THIS REFRESHING SUMMER SALAD
FEATURES ASIAN FLAVORS.

CAULIFLOWER AU GRATIN WITH CURED HAM

4 servings

1 large head of cauliflower, separated into florets

2 tablespoons butter

1 tablespoon all-purpose flour

½ cup (4 fl oz/125 ml) whole milk

¾ cup (6 oz/185 g) grated gruyère, swiss, or emmentaler cheese

½ cup (4 oz/125 g) grated monterey jack or white cheddar cheese

salt and freshly cracked pepper

10 slices of cured ham, chopped into small bits

1 tablespoon chives, finely chopped

Pour about 1 inch (2.5 cm) of water into a saucepan and bring to a boil. Place a steamer over the boiling water, add the cauliflower to the steamer, cover the pan, and steam until fork-tender, 4–6 minutes. In a separate saucepan, melt the butter and stir in the flour. Whisk in the milk little by little, stirring constantly to avoid clumps. Add the cheeses and mix well. Add more milk as needed to thin the sauce. Season the sauce with salt and pepper. Place the cauliflower, heads up, in a nonstick baking pan and pour the sauce over the top. While the cauliflower bakes, fry the ham in a dry pan until it becomes crispy. Sprinkle the ham and chives over the top with a little extra pepper.

> THIS IS A REALLY GOOD DISH FOR KIDS. WE EAT FAR TOO LITTLE CAULIFLOWER. THIS DISH SHOULD DO THE TRICK.

POTATO SALAD WITH MUSTARD & DILL

4 servings

1 lb (16 oz/500 g) new potatoes

salt and freshly cracked pepper

2 tablespoons olive oil

2 tablespoons coarse-grain mustard

1 small red onion, finely chopped

1 tablespoon coarsely chopped dill

1 tablespoon lemon juice

Boil the potatoes in salted water until tender. Strain off the water and cut the potatoes in half. Transfer them to a bowl. Mix together the oil, mustard, onion, dill, and lemon juice in a separate bowl. Pour the dressing over the potatoes and toss gently. Sprinkle salt and pepper to taste over the salad and serve while still hot.

SERVING TIP
This potato salad can be served hot or at room temperature.

HERE'S A FAST RECIPE FOR
A GREAT POTATO SALAD.

GRILLED CORN SOUP

4 servings

2 tablespoons butter

1 small onion, finely chopped

2 stalks celery, finely chopped

2 potatoes, peeled and cut into cubes

1 sprig thyme

½ cup (4 fl oz/125 g) chicken stock

grilled corn kernels cut from 3 ears of corn

1 cup (8 fl oz/250 g) heavy cream

salt and freshly cracked pepper

Melt the butter in a casserole dish and sauté the onion, celery, and potatoes until the onions become translucent and tender. Add the thyme and stock and cover the casserole with a lid. Let the soup simmer for 10 minutes. Add the corn and cream and let the soup simmer for an additional 10 minutes. Reserve a handful of kernels to garnish the top of the 4 soup servings. Pour the soup into a blender and purée until the mixture is smooth. Add salt and pepper to taste and serve with the garnish of corn kernels.

> THIS SOUP HAS A MILD SMOKY TASTE,
> WHICH COMPLEMENTS THE SWEET CORN.

CHAPTER 3
APPETIZERS

It was the big year for coming down with the measles. It was August and I was just about ready to start a new school year. New clothes were purchased and my hair was looking very smart. After only two days at school, I woke up one morning with my face and body covered with small red bumps. Measles. I became very ill with a high fever and crazy dreams. Mom explained that I had been babbling about food while the fever took its devastation. I talked about ingredients, how we should create a menu for a party, everything while I was far away from reality. I was especially preoccupied with oranges, though I'm not certain why. I couldn't remember much of this when I awoke. Dad bought all the Tintin books for me and he became my hero, which is why I have a Tintin tattoo on my left arm. After two months I was desperate to return to school with my friends, because it wasn't so much fun to sit in the window and watch other children play. When I was well, my whole family had a big party, which was called Paul's Fever Party. Family, friends, and school chums came and we ate, drank, and had a ball.

THIS PHENOMENAL RECIPE CAN BE USED AS A DIP, A TOPPING FOR LAMB OR CHICKEN, OR AS SALAD DRESSING.

FETA & LEMON DIP

4 servings

6½ oz (200 g) feta cheese, crumbled

1 tablespoon grated lemon zest, plus extra for garnish

2 tablespoons lemon juice

1 clove garlic, finely chopped

6 tablespoons (3 fl oz/90 ml) olive oil, plus more for serving

freshly cracked pepper

Combine the cheese, lemon zest, lemon juice, garlic, and oil in a blender or bowl and purée into a smooth dip. Spoon the dip into a serving bowl and drizzle some oil over the top along with pepper. Garnish with extra lemon zest. Serve with toasted rustic bread brushed with olive oil.

WATERMELON & CHILE SALSA

4 servings

¼ watermelon, peeled and seeds removed

1 fresh red chili, finely chopped

juice of 1 lime

¼ teaspoon red pepper flakes

2 tablespoons fresh cilantro, coarsely chopped

salt

Chop the watermelon into small cubes and place in a bowl. Add the fresh chile, lime juice, red pepper flakes, and cilantro. Mix well and add salt to taste. Refrigerate the salad for 1 hour before serving to marry the flavors.

SERVING TIP

You can serve this salsa with chips, as a topping for grilled fish or chicken, and in a composed salad.

THIS SALAD HAS A SPICY KICK
AND IS PERFECT FOR PICNICS

BAKED OYSTERS WITH SPINACH & BACON

12 pieces

4 strips bacon, chopped

3½ oz (105 g) spinach, roughly chopped

¼ teaspoon cayenne pepper

salt and freshly cracked pepper

12 raw oysters, opened and cleaned

Fry the bacon bits in a pan until brown and crispy. Add the spinach and stir until the leaves are wilted. Remove the pan from the heat and add the cayenne pepper. Add salt and pepper to taste. Top each oyster with the spinach mixture, dividing it evenly, and serve.

> HERE'S AN EVEN SIMPLER VARIATION OF OYSTERS ROCKEFELLER.

HALLOUMI WITH LEMON & APRICOTS

4 servings

6½ oz (200 g) halloumi or havarti cheese, cut in slabs

4 tablespoons (2 fl oz/60 ml) olive oil

zest from ½ lemon, finely chopped

1 tablespoon lemon juice

2 tablespoons finely chopped fresh dill

¼ teaspoon red pepper flakes

salt and freshly cracked pepper

12 apricots, halved

Grill the cheese in the middle of a hot grill and cook until golden, about 1 minute per side. Transfer to a platter. Whisk together the oil, lemon zest, lemon juice, dill, and red pepper flakes to make a dressing. Season with salt and pepper, then pour the dressing over the grilled cheese. Spread the apricots on the middle of the grill and cook until brown, about 1 minute per side. Transfer the fruit, skin-side down, to the plate with the cheese and serve.

HAVARTI AND HALLOUMI ARE AMONG THE BEST CHEESES TO GRILL. BOTH HAVE A SALTY TASTE AND ARE DELICIOUS WITH LEMON.

CRAB & CORN CAKES

4 servings

½ lb (250 g) fresh or canned crabmeat, drained and shredded

kernels from 1 ear of corn

½ cup (2 oz/60 g) breadcrumbs

½ cup (4 fl oz/125 ml) mayonnaise

1 tablespoon finely chopped fresh dill

1 large egg yolk

zest from ½ lemon, finely chopped

salt and freshly cracked pepper

canola oil, for frying

In a large bowl combine the crab, corn, breadcrumbs, mayonnaise, dill, egg yolk, lemon zest, and salt and pepper to taste. Heat about 1 inch (2.5 cm) of oil in a cast-iron pan. Using a tablespoon, scoop up spoonfuls of the crab mixture and carefully drop into the pan, one at a time, flattening the top to form a cake. Fry the crab cakes until golden brown, about 6 minutes per side. Transfer the cakes to paper towels to drain. Serve warm with tartar sauce.

GRILLED BABY BEETS WITH MUSTARD SAUCE

4 servings

6½ oz (200 g) halloumi cheese, sliced	2 tablespoons dijon mustard
16 baby beets, peeled and halved	1 teaspoon finely chopped fresh thyme
4 tablespoons (2 fl oz/60 ml) olive oil, plus more for brushing	1 tablespoon lemon juice
	salt
½ small onion, sliced into thin rings	
fresh dill sprigs, for garnish	

Brush the cheese slices and beets with oil. Place them in the middle of a hot grill and cook the cheese for about 1 minute per side and the beets for 3–4 minutes per side. Transfer the grilled cheese and beets to a platter. Top with the onion slices and garnish with dill sprigs. Whisk together the 4 tablespoons (2 fl oz/60 ml) oil, the Dijon, thyme, lemon juice, and salt to taste. Pour the dressing over the beet salad and serve.

COOKING TIP
You might want to wear rubber gloves when peeling the beets as they can stain. Don't wear white!

> HERE, SWEET GRILLED BEETS, SALTY CHEESE, AND AN ACIDIC DRESSING WORK TOGETHER PERFECTLY.

HOT CRAB DIP

4 servings

meat from 2 fresh dungeness crabs, picked through for shells

2 tablespoons mayonnaise

1 tablespoon lemon juice

1 tablespoon finely chopped fresh dill

1 teaspoon dijon mustard

salt and freshly cracked pepper

Combine the crab meat, mayonnaise, lemon juice, dill, Dijon, and salt and pepper to taste in a bowl and mix. Heat a dry nonstick pan over medium heat, then transfer the crab mixture into the pan, spreading it out. Cook until a fried crust forms on one side, about 5 minutes, then gently mix and continue to heat until the dip is heated through, about 3 minutes more. Spoon the warm dip into a bowl and serve with chips or crusty toast.

SERVING TIP
You can also use the empty rinsed crab shells as serving vessels for this dip.

THIS RECIPE IS FOOLPROOF. SOMETIMES I DECIDE TO TURN THE DIP INTO A CRAB CAKE—JUST CONTINUE TO COOK THE MIXTURE UNTIL IT IS NO LONGER RUNNY.

CORN & SHELLFISH FRITTERS WITH BASIL MAYONNAISE

4 servings

½ lb (250 g) small shrimp, crayfish, or langoustine, peeled

1 large egg

4 tablespoons (1 oz/30 g) breadcrumbs

2 green onions, finely chopped

1 tablespoon chopped fresh dill

salt and freshly cracked pepper

corn kernels from 2 boiled ears of corn

canola oil, for frying

1 cup (8 fl oz/250 mg) mayonnaise

2 tablespoons fresh basil, coarsely chopped

Place the shrimp, egg, breadcrumbs, green onions, dill, and salt and pepper to taste in a blender and purée until smooth. Add the corn kernels and blend again. Heat about 1 inch (2.5 cm) of oil in a cast-iron pan. The oil is hot enough when a few breadcrumbs thrown into the pan turn golden brown. Using a tablespoon, form the mixture in rounds and carefully set the rounded fritter into the hot oil. Repeat this process until the mixture is gone. Fry the fritters to a golden brown color. Combine the mayonnaise and basil in a small bowl. Serve the fritters hot with the basil mayonnaise.

SERVING TIP
Include the crayfish or langoustine shells as a garnish for a rustic touch.

PECORINO CHEESE & CHANTERELLE TART

4 servings

1 puff pastry sheet

all-purpose flour, for dusting

1 cup (4 oz/125 g) pecorino cheese, grated

3 tablespoons butter

3 cups (9 oz/270 g) chanterelle mushrooms, brushed clean

salt and freshly cracked pepper

1 tablespoon fresh rosemary leaves

2 tablespoons olive oil

Preheat the oven to 425°F (220°C). Line a baking sheet with parchment paper. Sprinkle some flour on a clean surface and roll out the puff pastry until it is double its original size. Transfer the pastry to the prepared baking sheet and sprinkle the top with the cheese. Melt the butter in a frying pan over medium heat, add the chanterelles, and sauté until golden brown, about 6 minutes. Spoon the sautéed chanterelles over the puff pastry. Sprinkle with salt, pepper, and the rosemary and drizzle with the oil. Bake the tart until it is golden brown, about 12 minutes, and serve.

THIS DISH IS EASY TO MAKE AND CAN BE SERVED HOT OR AT ROOM TEMPERATURE.

FOR A FUN SERVING IDEA, SERVE SANDWICHES THE WAY YOU WOULD CUT SLICES OF CAKE.

SANDWICH CAKE

4 servings

1 round loaf rustic bread

2 tablespoons pesto

leaves from 1 small head butter lettuce

3 ripe tomatoes, sliced

6 oz (180 g) whole mozzarella cheese, thinly sliced

10 thin slices ham

7 oz (220 g) oil-packed roasted red peppers, sliced

Slice the loaf of bread in half widthwise. Carefully remove most of the doughy center from both the top and bottom. (You can use this bread for breadcrumbs or dumplings.) Spread the pesto on the bottom piece and layer the lettuce leaves, tomato slices, cheese, ham, and peppers over the surface. Cover with the top piece of bread. Cut the sandwich into 4 wedges and serve.

SERVING TIP

Use any of your favorite sandwich fillings in this recipe.

SALMON CAVIAR WITH SOUR CREAM

4 servings

6 oz (200 g) sliced smoked salmon, finely chopped

1 small red onion, finely chopped

2 tablespoons finely chopped fresh dill

white pepper, for seasoning

¾ cup (6 oz/180 g) sour cream

4 tablespoons (2 oz/60 g) caviar

In a bowl combine the salmon, onion, dill, and white pepper to taste, and mix well. Divide the salmon mixture between 4 small glasses or bowls. Spoon some sour cream over each serving and top with the caviar.

VARIATIONS

You can substitute smoked trout or tuna for the smoked salmon.

THIS IS A QUICK LITTLE DISH, PERFECT FOR EVERYONE WHO LOVES SMOKED SALMON.

MUSSELS GRATINÉE

4 servings

2 lb (32 oz/1 kg) mussels, washed and cleaned

½ cup (4 fl oz/125 mg) dry white wine

6 cups (6 oz/180 g) spinach

½ cup (4 oz/125 g) breadcrumbs

½ cup (4 oz/125 g) butter

1 clove garlic, finely chopped

1 cup (4 oz/125 g) grated parmesan

Combine the mussels and wine in a large pot and bring to a boil over medium heat. Cook, covered, until the shells have opened up, about 3–4 minutes. Drain. Remove the mussels from the shells and reserve both the meat and shells. Meanwhile, pour about 1 inch (2.5 cm) of water into a saucepan and bring to a boil. Place a steamer over the boiling water, add the spinach to the steamer, cover the pan, and steam until wilted, 1–2 minutes. Drain and chop the spinach. Combine the breadcrumbs, butter, and garlic in a mixing bowl and stir. Rinse the shells. Place some spinach and breadcrumb mixture in each shell and layer with a mussel and finish with some Parmesan. Transfer the filled shells to a nonstick baking pan. Broil the mussels in a hot oven until the tops turn golden brown.

SERVING TIP
Cover the baking pan with sea salt and nestle the shells in the salt to stabalize them during cooking.

CHAPTER 4
DRINKS

Every Saturday morning, Mom and I would check out the food section in the newspaper. There was an article about how drinking homemade juice is very healthy. So we decided to buy a juicing machine. On the way home we stopped at a produce store and purchased tomatoes, celery, beets, carrots—everything healthy ended up in the basket. We arrived home, unpacked the goods, and pondered how to change our lives. I must say that the machine was quite impressive, all stainless steel with a multitude of buttons. What followed was nothing short of a black comedy. The machine began to rumble. We looked at one another and let out a great scream when it began to leak. Suddenly there was a bang and the whole room was covered in tomatoes, celery, and cucumber. We're talking the whole kitchen covered in juice! I can still recall how we broke down with laughter for 15 minutes before we began cleaning up the mess. The machine was brought down to the basement and has never again seen the light of day.

APRICOT & ROSEMARY MIMOSAS

4 servings

⅓ cup (3 oz/9 mg) sugar

1 sprig fresh rosemary

2 ripe apricots, peeled, pitted, and halved

sparkling wine, for topping

Combine ½ cup (4 fl oz/125 mg) water, the sugar, and rosemary in a small pot and bring to a boil. Stir the mixture until the sugar dissolves, then cool in the refrigerator. Remove the rosemary and pour the sugar syrup into a blender. Add the apricots and purée the mixture until smooth. Divide the apricot purée evenly between 4 glasses and top with sparkling wine.

HERE'S MY VARIATION OF A MIMOSA,
MADE WITH A HINT OF FRESH ROSEMARY.

CHERRY LEMONADE FOR ADULTS

about 20 servings

1 cup (8 fl oz/250 ml) lemon juice

6½ oz (200 g) fresh cherries, pitted

¾ cup (6 oz/185 g) sugar

dark rum, for topping

sparkling water, for topping

Combine the lemon juice and cherries in a blender and purée until smooth. Pour the lemon mixture into a pot and add ¾ cup (6 fl oz/180 ml) water and the sugar. Simmer over medium heat and stir until the sugar dissolves. For a nonalcoholic version, let the cherry lemonade cool, then pour the drink in glasses, top with sparkling water, and serve. For the adult version, add 1 jigger (3 tablespoons) of rum to each glass of cherry lemonade and top with sparkling water.

THIS DRINK IS A LITTLE DANGEROUS. YOU DON'T REALIZE YOU'RE DRINKING A COCKTAIL, BUT JUST WAIT UNTIL YOU STAND UP.

PAUL'S WATERMELON COOLER

1 serving

4 chunks of watermelon, seeded

1 jigger (3 tablespoons) simple syrup (page 132)

1 jigger (3 tablespoons) gin

2 tablespoons aperol

2 tablespoons lemon juice

crushed ice

sparkling water, for topping

Combine the watermelon and simple syrup in a cocktail shaker and muddle with a pestle until well mixed. Add the gin, Aperol, lemon juice, and ice. Cover and shake well. Pour the cocktail into a tall glass and top the drink with sparkling water.

I BEGAN TO MAKE THIS NEW VARIATION OF A COCKTAIL ONE SUMMER WHEN I ACQUIRED A LARGE WATERMELON FROM A FRIEND AND CAME UP WITH LOTS OF WAYS TO IT.

RED SANGRIA

1 large pitcher, about 8 servings

1 bottle dry red wine

½ cup (4 fl oz/125 ml) cointreau

¾ cup (6 fl oz/180 mg) orange juice

½ cup (4 fl oz/125 ml) lemon juice

¾ cup (6 oz/185 g) simple syrup (see below)

1 orange, sliced

1 lemon, sliced

1 lime, sliced

ice cubes

Combine the red wine, Cointreau, orange juice, lemon juice, simple syrup, citrus slices, and ice cubes in a large pitcher and serve.

COOKING TIP

Simple syrup, sometimes called sugar syrup, is just equal parts water and sugar brought to a boil until the sugar dissolves, and then cooled. Use it to sweeten cocktails, lemonade, or ice tea.

BLOODY MATHILDA

1 pitcher, about 4 servings

2 large tomatoes

½ cup (4 fl oz/125 ml) vodka

½ cup (4 fl oz/125 ml) beef broth

½ cup (4 fl oz/125 ml) lemon juice

a few dashes worcestershire sauce

1 tablespoon fresh horseradish, finely grated

1 teaspoon tabasco sauce

celery stalks, for garnish

Using a fork, mash the tomatoes in a large bowl. Remove as much water from the fruit as possible, straining the tomato liquid into a pitcher. Add the vodka, beef broth, lemon juice, Worcestershire, horseradish, and Tabasco, and mix. Pour into glasses and garnish each serving with a celery stalk.

THIS VERSION OF A BLOODY MARY IS A LITTLE MILDER AND MORE ELEGANT THAN THE CLASSIC RECIPE. MAKE SURE THE TOMATOES ARE PERFECTLY RIPE.

Summer Food / Drinks

GREEN GIANT

1 serving

1 tablespoon fresh cilantro, chopped

2 celery stalks

2 jiggers (6 tablespoons) simple syrup
  (page 132)

2 jiggers (6 tablespoons) lime juice

1 cup (8 fl oz/250 ml) tequila

ice

Combine the cilantro and 1 stalk celery in a blender and crush down the celery with a muddler. Add the simple syrup, lime juice, and tequila. Fill the blender with ice and purée until smooth. Strain the drink into a glass and garnish with the remaining celery.

A COCKTAIL WITH THE NAME ANNEFRID

1 serving

4 blackberries or boysenberries

5 blueberries

4 raspberries

1 sprig fresh rosemary

juice from ½ lime

3 tablespoons simple syrup (page 132)

2 jiggers (6 tablespoons) vodka, or to taste

ice cubes

sparkling water, for topping

Combine the berries in a cocktail shaker and mash well with a muddler. Add the rosemary, lime juice, simple syrup, vodka, and ice cubes. Shake the drink thoroughly and fill a glass. Top with sparkling water.

I MADE THIS BERRY COCKTAIL FOR A SUMMER PARTY YEARS AGO AND IT'S BEEN POPULAR SINCE.

STRAWBERRY MARGARITAS

2 servings

1 pint (8 oz/250 g) strawberries, cleaned

1 tablespoon sugar

¼ cup (2 fl oz/60 ml) tequila

1 jigger (3 tablespoons) triple sec

juice from 2 limes

ice cubes

Combine the strawberries, sugar, and ¼ cup (2 fl oz/60 ml) water in a pot and bring to a boil. Let the mixture simmer for about 25 minutes, or until the strawberries are completely softened, then cool to room temperature. Transfer the mixture to a blender and add the tequila, Triple Sec, lime juice and ice and purée to a smooth and even consistency. Pour into individual glasses and serve.

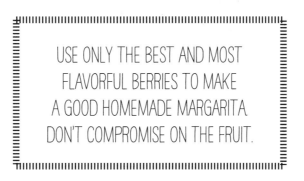

USE ONLY THE BEST AND MOST
FLAVORFUL BERRIES TO MAKE
A GOOD HOMEMADE MARGARITA.
DON'T COMPROMISE ON THE FRUIT.

PIMM'S CUP

1 serving

ice cubes

2 strawberries, halved lengthwise

1 slice lemon

1 slice lime

1 thin slice cucumber, cut lengthwise

2 jiggers (6 tablespoons) pimm's no. 1

3 tablespoons fresh orange juice

ginger ale, for topping

Fill a large glass with ice, then add the strawberries, lemon, lime, and cucumber. Pour the Pimm's and orange juice into the glass and top with ginger ale.

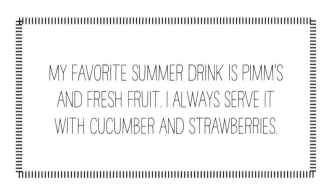

MY FAVORITE SUMMER DRINK IS PIMM'S AND FRESH FRUIT. I ALWAYS SERVE IT WITH CUCUMBER AND STRAWBERRIES.

CHAPTER 5

MAIN COURSES

The best part of summer is that one can cook and enjoy eating food outdoors. I think it's amazing to stand in front of the barbecue and turn the meat or fish over, resulting in a perfect temperature. I never stand alone, which is something I learned from my father. I always stand with my friend, GT, or gin and tonic, as it is called. Otherwise it can be a little lonely. Is there anything better than the taste of grilled food?

A simple hot dog becomes a culinary delight after it has spent a little time on the barbecue. There are simple rules to follow in order to appreciate a grilled meal. On the next page you will find my six best tips.

PAUL'S 6 GRILLING TIPS

GAS VS. CHARCOAL

I like using a gas grill best, because it's easy to regulate the heat to get the most even results. It's also easy to use indirect heat, meaning the heat comes from the sides and not just underneath. Indirect-heat grilling is perfect for cooking a whole chicken or a large cut of meat.

NOTHING COLD ON THE GRILL

Meat, fish, and poultry, and even vegetables, should be room temperature before going on the grill. Placing cold items on the grill will dry out the food during cooking.

MARINATE

Marinate what you grill. A good marinade will elevate the most ordinary piece of meat to a heavenly state of flavor. A little olive oil, soy sauce, garlic, and herbs is ample. Let meat marinate for at least one hour.

SPRAY BOTTLE

When you grill something with fat, like a sirloin steak or pork chop, it's great to have a spray bottle with clear water nearby. If the meat becomes aflame because of the fat, just spray the grill with a little water and everything will be all right again.

OIL THE GRILL

Fish tastes wonderful grilled, but it can be a little tricky to work with—a whole fish can fall apart during cooking. To prevent this from happening, brush the grill rack with oil before placing fish on the grill.

FUN

Have fun with grilling and try new things. Did you know that you can grill a pizza? See page 46. You can bake cakes, steam mussels, and do so much more. Use your imagination when grilling.

HALLOUMI, BASIL & PROSCIUTTO CHICKEN

4 servings

4 chicken breasts, skinless

olive oil, for coating

salt and freshly cracked pepper

12 basil leaves

4 slices prosciutto di Parma

8 slices halloumi cheese

Preheat the oven to 350°F (180°C). Cut each chicken breast in half lengthwise, keeping the bottom attached and leaving a cavity for stuffing from the top. Rub each chicken breast well with oil, salt, and pepper. Stuff each piece with 3 basil leaves, 1 piece of prosciutto, and 2 slices of cheese. Bind together the open chicken cavity with kitchen twine. Lay the wrapped chicken on a nonstick baking pan with a splash of oil over the top. Roast the chicken to a golden brown color, about 18 minutes. Transfer the chicken to individual plates and let them rest for 5 minutes before serving.

SERVING TIP
You can also stuff the chicken with mozzarella cheese.

THIS EASY OVEN-ROASTED DISH
IS DELICIOUS ACCOMPANIED BY
ROASTED POTATOES WITH FRESH HERBS.

PORK TENDERLOIN FILLET IN TOMATO & MUSHROOM SAUCE

4 servings

1½ lb (750 g) pork tenderloin	2 cans whole tomatoes
salt and freshly cracked pepper	1 tablespoon finely chopped
olive oil, for coating	fresh basil, plus whole leaves
1 cup (3 oz/90 g) mushrooms, sliced	for garnish
4 shallots, finely chopped	8 oz (250 g) mozzarella cheese,
2 cloves garlic, finely chopped	sliced

Trim the pork of fat and rub it with salt and pepper. Heat a pan lightly coated in oil and brown the pork on all sides. Remove the pork from the pan and transfer to a cutting board to rest. Add the mushrooms to the pan and sauté until browned on both sides. Remove the mushrooms from the pan and reserve. Fry the shallots and garlic in the pan. Pass the tomatoes through a sieve to remove the seeds and skin and add the tomato juice to the pan along with the chopped basil. Mix the sauce well, bring to a boil, and simmer for 5 minutes. Slice the pork into pieces ¾ inch (2 cm) thick and set the slices in the sauce. Cover the pork with cheese and sprinkle the mushrooms over the top. Cover the pan with a lid and cook over low heat, 15–20 minutes. Serve with basil leaves sprinkled over the top.

SERVING TIP

Serve this dish with steamed rice or a potato purée.

> THIS FLAVORFUL RECIPE IS A GREAT CHOICE FOR A DINNER PARTY.

LEMON & CHILI MARINATED SALMON FILLET

4 servings

zest from 1 lemon, finely chopped

juice from 1 lemon

2 tablespoons soy sauce

¼ teaspoon red pepper flakes

1 tablespoon mirin

¼ teaspoon salt

1½ lb (24 oz/750 g) salmon filet, skinned

olive oil, for coating

asian cucumber salad (page 42)

Whisk together the lemon zest, lemon juice, soy sauce, red pepper flakes, mirin, and salt in a small bowl. Place the fish on a platter and pour the marinade over the top. Leave the fish to marinate, turning it over every 30 minutes. Grease one side of a large piece of aluminum foil with oil and lay the fish on the top. Discard the marinade. Securely pack the fish in the foil and set the pack on the grill with high indirect heat. Cook for 18–20 minutes. Open the pack and serve the salmon with the cucumber salad.

COOKING TIP

Indirect heat refers to the cooking method of heating the food from the sides, rather than from directly underneath. With this method the temperature is regulated and the food is less likely to burn.

SALMON COOKED ON THE GRILL
IS TERRIFIC. I GRILL THIS DISH
USING ALUMINUM FOIL.

FRESH THYME & TOMATO MUSSELS

4 servings

2 tablespoons olive oil

1 small onion, finely chopped

2 shallots, finely chopped

2 cloves garlic, finely chopped

4 lbs (2 kg) fresh mussels, rinsed and cleaned

1 sprig fresh thyme

½ cup (4 fl oz/125 ml) dry white wine

½ cup (4 fl oz/125 ml) chicken stock

2 cups (12 oz/375 g) cherry tomatoes

salt and freshly cracked pepper

Heat the oil in a large pot. Add the onion, shallots, and garlic to the pot and sauté until the onion is translucent and tender. Add the mussels, thyme, wine, stock, and tomatoes to the pot and cover with a lid, cooking 3–4 minutes. Stir the mixture well, circulating the shells throughout various levels. Pluck out and discard any shells that do not open. Season the mussels with salt and pepper to taste. Ladle the mussels and broth into large soup bowls.

IF THIS ISN'T THE TASTE OF SUMMER, I DON'T KNOW WHAT IS. SERVE WITH GOOD CRUSTY BREAD AND AN EVEN BETTER BOTTLE OF WHITE WINE.

GRILLED FISH & CORN TORTILLAS

4 servings

1¼ lbs (20 oz/625 g) cod fillet, skin removed	2 large tomatoes, seeded and cut into small cubes
2 ears of corn	½ red onion, thinly sliced
1 teaspoon salt	1 green spring onion, coarsely chopped
2 teaspoons red pepper flakes	
olive oil, for coating	a small bunch of fresh cilantro, coarsely chopped
8 corn tortillas, small–medium size	
1 small head (¼ lb/125 g) butter lettuce, shredded into small pieces	juice from 1 lime

Rub the fish and corn with olive oil, the salt, and red pepper flakes. Grill the fish for 12–15 minutes in the center of a medium-hot grill, or until the fish is cooked through and has a flaky consistency. Transfer the fish to a plate and break the fish into bite-sized bits with two forks. The corn should be grilled for about 2 minutes on each side to achieve an overall brown color. Use a sharp knife to slice the corn from the cob, cutting lengthwise from top to bottom. Warm the tortillas on the grill, cooking for less than 1 minute on each side, just to heat them slightly. Fill the tortillas with lettuce, fish, tomatoes, red onion, green onion, and cilantro. Drizzle a little oil and lime juice over the top of the filling and serve.

COOKING TIP

When you grill the fish, it is wise to use a fish rack. This way the fish won't burn and it is easy to turn. A smart investment!

THIS FAVORITE SUMMER SALAD
IS ALSO GOOD MADE
WITH SALMON OR TROUT.

SALAD WITH COD & RED BEETS WITH DILL VINAIGRETTE

4 servings

6 red beets	**VINAIGRETTE**
20 small new potatoes, halved	½ cup (4 fl oz/125 ml) olive oil
13 oz (410 g) fresh cod fillets, skinned	1 teaspoon fresh dill, finely chopped
	juice from ½ lemon
salt and freshly cracked pepper	
2 tablespoons olive oil	
2 oz (60 g) capers	
grated lemon zest from 1 lemon	
a small bunch of fresh dill sprigs	

Preheat the oven to 400°F (200°C). Peel the beets and cut them in boat-shaped pieces. Place the beets, potatoes, and cod in a nonstick baking pan. Sprinkle the fish and vegetables with salt and pepper. Drizzle the oil over the top. Roast the vegetables in the oven until tender and the fish is cooked through. The fish is finished cooking when it begins to flake. The fish will cook before the vegetables, so remove when cooked, and reserve. Break the fish into bite-sized bits with two forks. Serve the fish with the potatoes and red beets, along with the capers and lemon zest on individual plates. Whisk all the ingredients for the vinaigrette together thoroughly in a small bowl, season with salt and pepper, and pour it in equal parts over each salad. Garnish the salads with dill sprigs.

PASTA WITH SMOKED SALMON & LEMON

4 servings

1 tablespoon grated lemon zest

2 tablespoons lemon juice

4 tablespoons (2 fl oz/60 ml) olive oil

13 oz (410 g) spaghetti, cooked al dente

6½ oz (200 g) smoked salmon, cut in sliced bite-sized bits

a small bunch of fresh dill sprigs

salt and freshly cracked pepper

Whisk the lemon zest, lemon juice, and oil together in a small bowl. Pour the dressing over the spaghetti, divided equally between 4 plates, and toss well. Add the smoked salmon and dill to each plate. Sprinkle salt and pepper over the top to taste.

VARIATIONS
If you desire a more pronounced flavor, you can add capers or red pepper flakes.

SHRIMP WITH GREEN PEPPER & GARLIC

4 servings

12–16 large shrimp

2 cloves garlic, finely chopped

1 tablespoon whole green peppercorns in brine, finely chopped

1 teaspoon ground cumin

2 fresh green chiles, finely chopped

½ teaspoon salt

¼ lb (4 oz/125 g) butter

4 lemon wedges

Rinse and devein the shrimp, but you can leave the shells on, if desired. Mix the garlic, peppercorns, cumin, chiles, and salt together. Melt the butter in a pan and sauté the shrimp over medium-high heat for 1 minute. Turn the shrimp and pour over the spice mixture. Mix the ingredients together and serve hot with lemon wedges.

THIS IS PURE COMFORT FOOD
AND MAKES A GREAT APPETIZER.

CHICKEN LEGS WITH OLIVES & LEMON

4 servings

8 chicken legs

salt and freshly cracked pepper

2 tablespoons olive oil

juice from 1 lemon

1 lemon, cut into wedges

2 tablespoons capers

a small bunch of fresh basil leaves

Rub the chicken with salt and pepper. Warm the oil in a pan and brown the chicken on each side over medium-high heat. Transfer the chicken to a nonstick baking pan. Pour the lemon juice over the chicken, add the lemon wedges and capers, and bake in a preheated oven at 350°F (180°C), for 12–15 minutes. Sprinkle fresh basil leaves over the top before serving.

SALMON WORKS SUPERBLY FOR BURGERS.
HERE, THE TASTY CAPERS ADD
A WELCOME SALTY KICK.

SALMON BURGERS

4 servings

1¼ lb (20 oz/625 g) salmon fillets, skinless

½ cup (2 oz/60 g) breadcrumbs

1 large egg

2 tablespoons fresh dill, coarsely chopped

1 large shallot, coarsely chopped

1 tablespoon capers, coarsely chopped

1 teaspoon salt

½ teaspoon freshly cracked pepper

2 tablespoons olive oil

8 slices toasted bread

8 slices fresh tomato

1 English cucumber, sliced

mayonnaise, for serving

Cut the salmon into bits. Place the salmon, breadcrumbs, egg, dill, shallot, capers, salt, and pepper into a food processor and pulse into a smooth mixture. Form 4 large burgers from the mixture with wet hands. Cool the burgers in the refrigerator for 1 hour. Brush the surfaces of the burgers with the oil. Place the burgers in the center of a hot grill and cook them for 2–4 minutes on each side until browned. Serve the burgers on the toasted bread with 2 slices of tomato, some cucumber slices, and mayonnaise.

VARIATIONS
You can blend together various types of fish for burgers, and also use shrimp, crayfish, or crabmeat.

KICK-ASS SCAMPI

4 servings

30 small cooked (cocktail) shrimp, deveined and cleaned

4 tablespoons (2 oz/60 g) melted butter

4 tablespoons (2 fl oz/60 ml) Asian-style sweet chili sauce

1 tablespoon apple cider vinegar

8 lemon wedges

Place the shrimp on the grill, and grill for about 1 minute on each side, depending on the size of the shrimp. Mix together the butter, chili sauce, and vinegar in a bowl. As soon as the shrimp are ready, transfer the shrimp into the mixture and toss well. Serve the shrimp hot with lemon wedges.

THIS MAKES A NICE LIGHT LUNCH OR SNACK.
YOU CAN ALSO USE JUMBO SHRIMP.

LAMB MEAT WORKS WELL FOR BURGERS.
USE GROUND CUMIN WITH THE LAMB
TO GIVE THE BURGERS AN EXOTIC TASTE.

LAMB BURGERS WITH MINT & FETA PESTO

4 servings

MINT & FETA PESTO

makes 1 cup (8 oz/250 g)

26 oz (815 g) ground lamb

1 tablespoon shallot, finely chopped

1 tablespoon fresh mint, finely chopped

1 clove garlic, pressed

1 teaspoon salt

½ teaspoon freshly cracked pepper

½ teaspoon ground cumin

2 tablespoons olive oil

4 pita pockets

mint and feta pesto (see right)

Mix together the lamb, shallot, mint, garlic, and spices in a bowl. Form 4 large oval-shaped burgers. Brush the surfaces of the burgers with the oil. Place the burgers in the center of a hot grill. Cook the burgers for approximately 4 minutes on each side. Set the pitas on the grill to warm and brown the surfaces. Slice the pita breads at the top, slip a burger halfway into each pita, and serve with the mint and feta pesto.

1⅓ cups (7½ oz/200 g) crumbled feta cheese

4 tablespoons olive oil

2 tablespoons fresh mint, finely chopped

2 tablespoons roasted pine nuts,
   finely chopped

¼ teaspoon dried red pepper flakes

salt and freshly cracked pepper

Mix all the ingredients in a small bowl and season with salt and pepper. Leave the mixture to stand for 1 hour at room temperature prior to serving, so that the flavors balance harmoniously.

> GREAT WITH EVERYTHING! THAT'S IT!

CHILE & LIME CHICKEN

4 servings

1 whole chicken, rinsed and cleaned under cold water

juice from 2 limes, plus lime halves for serving

3 tablespoons olive oil

1 teaspoon red pepper flakes

salt, for sprinkling

Cut the chicken into pieces with a sharp knife and poultry shears. Whisk together the lime juice, oil, and red pepper flakes in a small bowl. Rub the mixture well onto the chicken pieces. Sprinkle the chicken with salt. Place the chicken onto the center of a hot grill and cook indirectly, about 20 minutes. You can also roast the chicken in a preheated 350°F (180°C) oven, about 20 minutes.

Place some additional lime halves on the grill and squeeze the juice over the top of the chicken just before serving.

THIS CHICKEN HAS DELICIOUS FLAVOR FROM THE CHILE AND LIME JUICE, WHICH ALSO HELPS TENDERIZE THE MEAT.

SPARERIBS

4 servings

4 lbs (2 kg) spareribs

1¼ cups (10 fl oz/310 ml) bbq sauce (page 175)

1 tablespoon Worcestershire sauce

¼ cup (2 oz/60 g) light brown sugar, firmly packed

grated zest from 1 lemon

2 teaspoons dried red pepper flakes

Bring a large pot of water to a boil. Lay the spareribs in the pot and cook for 20 minutes. Remove the ribs from the pot, place them in a bowl, and leave to cool at room temperature. Bring all the remaining ingredients to a boil in a small pot, stirring the mixture vigorously until the sugar is dissolved. Pour the sauce over the meat and rub the sauce over all the surfaces. Grill the spareribs on the center of a hot grill, cooking them for approximately 2–3 minutes on each side, until the sugar in the sauce caramelizes and turns a deep brown color.

THIS IS A MUST-HAVE RECIPE. WITH SPARERIBS THE MEAT SHOULD JUST FALL OFF THE BONE.

SUPER EASY AND SO GOOD. YOU CAN
MAKE YOUR OWN BBQ SAUCE
OR USE A READY-MADE VERSION.

BBQ CHICKEN

4 servings

1 large free-range organic chicken,

   cut into quarters

1 batch BBQ sauce

Rinse the chicken and clean the cavity under cold running water. Dry the remaining moisture from the chicken with paper towels. Cut away any excess fat from the chicken. Place the chicken in the center of a hot grill, over indirect heat. After about 10 minutes, begin brushing all sides of the chicken with the BBQ sauce. Be generous with the sauce, because that's where the taste lies. Stick a knife in the thickest part of the leg. When the juice bubbles out clear in color, the chicken is finished cooking. Serve with extra BBQ sauce.

MY BBQ SAUCE

makes about 1 cup (8 oz/250 g)

2 tablespoons olive oil

1 small whole onion, finely chopped

1 clove garlic, finely chopped

zest from ½ lemon, finely chopped

juice from ½ lemon

½ cup (3½ oz/105 g) dark brown sugar,

   firmly packed

¼ cup (2 fl oz/60 ml) apple cider vinegar

½ cup (4 fl oz/125 ml) ketchup

1 tablespoon Worcestershire sauce

½ teaspoon Tabasco sauce

½ teaspoon cayenne pepper (optional)

Heat the oil in a pan and sauté the onion and garlic until they are tender and translucent. Add the remaining ingredients, stir, and simmer for 10 minutes. Cool the sauce to room temperature and store the remaining amount for up to 3 weeks in the fridge.

> I'VE MADE THIS SAUCE FOR YEARS AND IT GETS BETTER EACH TIME—IT'S SUPER FOR CHICKEN, MEAT, AND FISH.

PORK CHOPS WITH BALSAMIC FIGS

4 servings

½ cup (4 fl oz/125 ml) balsamic vinegar

3 tablespoons sugar

10 figs, halved

1 bay leaf

4 large pork chops, boneless (if preferred)

olive oil, for coating

salt and freshly cracked pepper

¼ teaspoon red pepper flakes

Combine the balsamic vinegar and sugar in a small pot and bring to a boil. When the sugar has dissolved, add the figs and bay leaf. Heat the mixture to a thick consistency, 5–6 minutes. While the sauce is still hot, rub the pork with some oil, and season with salt, pepper, and the red pepper flakes. Make small incisions with a knife around the perimeter of fat on the pork chop to prevent curling of the meat while cooking. Grill the chops in the middle of a hot grill for about 4 minutes on each side. Transfer the pork to plates and serve with the balsamic figs.

THIS IS THE PERFECT PARTY FOOD.

MACKEREL WITH SUMMER CABBAGE

4 servings

4 whole mackerel, preferably the small young, variety

2 tablespoons olive oil

salt and freshly cracked pepper

1 lemon, thinly sliced

1 small bunch fresh dill, coarsely chopped

2 tablespoons butter

2 tablespoons mirin

¼ teaspoon sugar

2 small summer cabbages (pointed leaf top variety), sliced in chiffonade

Rinse the fish under cold water. Rub the fish with the oil inside the cavity and out. Sprinkle salt and pepper inside the cavity of the fish. Stuff the cavity with lemon and dill and place the mackerel in a fish rack. Place the fish at the center of a hot grill and cook for 12–14 minutes, turning the rack now and then so that the fish doesn't burn. Heat the butter, mirin, and sugar in a pan and sauté the cabbage until it is tender and loosens into soft curly strips. Serve the cabbage hot with the whole fish.

COOKING TIP
Use a fish rack when grilling the fish. Grease the rack with oil first, so that the fish doesn't stick while cooking.

I HAVE MANY CHILDHOOD MEMORIES OF DAD'S GRILLED MACKEREL FROM OUR SUMMER COTTAGE IN SANDEFJORD.

GRILLED GREEK KEBAB

4 servings

10 oz (310 g) tender lamb meat, cut in bite-sized pieces

3 tablespoons rub for the lamb (page 183)

3 small red onions, cut into small wedges

rosemary sprigs, for garnish

2 tablespoons olive oil

1 lemon, cut into wedges

Mix the lamb thoroughly with the rub in a mixing bowl. Alternate piercing 3 pieces of lamb and 3 wedges of onion through the centers on wooden skewers. Place some of the rosemary sprigs in between the bite-sized pieces, or alternatively use long rosemary twigs as the skewers. Brush the kebabs with the oil. Place the kebabs in the center of a hot grill, turning them often to brown all the surfaces, 8–9 minutes. Squeeze the lemon juice over the top before serving hot.

COOKING TIP
If you use wooden or rosemary twig skewers, you should always soak them in water for 1 hour before grilling. If not, they will burn.

> KEBABS ARE ALWAYS FUN TO MAKE.
> YOU CAN USE ALL THE VEGETABLES YOU
> LIKE BEST. NO RULES HERE; ANYTHING GOES!

RUB FOR LAMB

makes about ½ cup (4 oz/125 g)

2 tablespoons coriander seeds

1 tablespoon cumin seeds

2 teaspoons mustard seeds

½ teaspoon whole cardamom

1 tablespoon salt

2 teaspoons dry ginger powder

1 teaspoon red pepper flakes

½ teaspoon ground nutmeg

Heat a dry pan and cook the coriander, cumin, mustard, and cardamom until the seeds darken in color and exude a strong aroma. Cool the mixture to room temperature, mix with the remaining ingredients, and pulse in a spice grinder. Blend the ingredients into a powder. Store in a glass jar or plastic container in a cool pantry space. The rub will keep up to 6 months.

A HOMEMADE BURGER TASTES SO MUCH
BETTER THAN PRE-FORMED ONES YOU
BUY IN A STORE. THEY ARE MUCH
JUICIER AND MORE DELICIOUS.

BURGER

4 servings

2 lb (1 kg) lean ground beef

3 tablespoons onion, finely chopped

2 tablespoons ketchup

a few drops of Worcestershire sauce

1 teaspoon salt

½ teaspoon freshly cracked pepper

2 tablespoons olive oil

4 slices cheese, preferably Jarlsberg or Cheddar

butter lettuce leaves, mayonnaise, and grilled onion slices, for garnish

4 hamburger buns, toasted

Carefully mix the beef, onion, ketchup, Worcestershire, salt, and pepper in a mixing bowl. With wet hands, form 4 large burgers. Brush the surface of the burgers with the oil. Place the burgers at the center of a hot grill and cook for 3-4 minutes on each side. After you have turned the burger over, place a slice of cheese on top. Serve the burgers with mayonnaise, lettuce, and grilled onions on a toasted bun.

COOKING TIP

Don't overmix the meat: just mix so that the ingredients are integrated and it holds together. If you mix the meat too much, the burgers become dry, and we can't have that, can we?

GRILLED PORK TENDERLOIN WITH SALSA VERDE

4 servings

3 tablespoons fresh flat-leaf parsley, roughly chopped

2 tablespoons fresh mint leaves, roughly chopped

2 tablespoons fresh dill, roughly chopped

1 tablespoon Dijon mustard

1 teaspoon capers

¼ teaspoon red pepper flakes

4 tablespoons (2 fl oz/60 ml) olive oil

1 large tenderloin of pork, trimmed of fat

salt and freshly cracked pepper

Place the parsley, mint, dill, Dijon, capers, red pepper flakes, and 2 tablespoons olive oil in a small blender and pulse into a smooth and shiny sauce. Rub the pork with the remaining 2 tablespoons olive oil and season with salt and pepper. Lay the pork in the center of a hot grill and cook with indirect heat for 18–20 minutes, browning the pork on all sides. Transfer the pork to a cutting board and leave to rest for 10 minutes. Slice the pork and serve plated with sauce on the side or drizzled with a spoon over the meat.

> SALSA VERDE TASTES PERFECT WITH THE SLIGHT SWEETNESS OF PORK MEAT.

CHAPTER 6

DESSERTS

My grandmother was always my greatest inspiration when it came to cooking. She never wrote a recipe down on paper, but managed to contain it all in her head. I'm upset that I never wrote down her recipes before she passed away. I grew up in a home with a large garden, which was full of fruit trees, berry bushes, and masses of flowers. It was Grandmother who ruled the garden domain. Her secret to get plants to grow to immense scale was chicken dung, which she received from a farmer who lived nearby. It didn't smell particularly great, but I promise you that the strawberries and raspberries were twice the size of our neighbors' crops. Every year in August, my family took a week's holiday to visit Grandmother for jam and juice week. She wouldn't let anyone in the house. She and my Aunt Gunvor picked everything from the garden and transformed it into jam, juice, chutney . . . the list goes on. We had juice and jam all winter. Before everything was picked, Grandmother would serve us the most fantastic buns with sun-ripened berries. With a little cream and sugar over the top, it was just like eating summer.

CRUMBLE PIE WITH SUMMER BERRIES

4 servings

4 pints (32 oz/1 kg) mixed berries, rinsed and dried

½ cup (4 oz/125 g) sugar

¼ teaspoon salt

1 teaspoon cornstarch

zest from 1 orange, grated

2 tablespoons fresh orange juice

4 tablespoons (2 oz/60 g) butter, softened

4 tablespoons (2 oz/60 g) brown sugar, firmly packed

1 cup (5 oz/155 g) all-purpose flour

Preheat the oven to 350°F (180°C). Pour the berries into a nonstick baking dish and toss with the sugar, salt, cornstarch, orange zest, and orange juice. Mix the butter, brown sugar, and flour together in a bowl and form crumbles with your fingers. Spread the crumble mixture over the fruit. Bake the crumble until golden brown in color, about 30 minutes. Cool until warm or room temperature and serve with sour cream or ice cream.

I REMEMBER MY GRANDMOTHER MAKING THIS ALL SUMMER, LEAVING ME WITH TRULY FOND MEMORIES OF LONG DAYS IN THE GARDEN.

WATERMELON & CHILE PALETAS

6 pieces

½ cup (4 oz/125 g) sugar

1 dried red chile

4 cups (32 fl oz/1 l) watermelon, seeds removed

2 tablespoons fresh lime juice

Combine ½ cup (4 fl oz/125 ml) water, sugar, and chile in a pot and bring to a boil. Whisk the sugar until it has dissolved. Remove the pot from the heat and remove the chile. Put half of the watermelon, the sugar syrup, and lime juice in a blender and pulse to purée. Add the remaining watermelon and continue to purée. Lay sticks in a popsicle mold and pour in the watermelon mixture. Freeze the popsicles overnight. When ready to enjoy, run warm water over the mold until the pops slide out.

VARIATIONS

You can substitute the watermelon with strawberries, raspberries, or mango.

PALETAS ARE MEXICAN ICE POPS, WHICH ARE FRUIT BASED AND SIMILAR TO SORBET.

GOOD OLD-FASHIONED BERRY SOUP–IT DOESN'T GET ANY MORE SUMMER THAN THIS.

SUMMER BERRY SOUP

4 servings

½ cup (4 oz/125 g) sugar

2 pints (16 oz/500 g) strawberries, cleaned and cut into bits

1 pint (8 oz/250 g) raspberries, cleaned, plus more for garnish

juice from 1–2 lemons

crème fraîche, for garnish

Combine 4 cups (32 fl oz/1 l) water, the sugar, berries, and lemon juice in a pot and bring to a boil and stir until the sugar is dissolved. Strain the soup through a sieve. This soup is best if it is chilled overnight in the refrigerator. Serve the soup chilled with a dollop of crème fraîche and some berries to garnish.

VARIATIONS

You can also substitute the strawberries and raspberries with blueberries, blackberries, or red currants.

BLUEBERRY PANCAKE CAKE

8 servings

1¼ cups (6¼ oz/200 g) all-purpose flour

2 cups (16 fl oz/500 ml) whole milk

1–2 tablespoons salt

½ cup (4 oz/125 g) sugar, plus 3 tablespoons

4 large eggs

butter, for frying

2 pints (16 oz/500 g) blueberries

1 teaspoon lime zest, grated

Mix together the flour, milk, salt, the 3 tablespoons sugar, and the eggs in a bowl. Set the bowl in the refrigerator and let the mixture chill for 20 minutes. Melt a scant amount of butter in an omelet-size pan and fry thin pancakes. This amount of mixture makes about 20 small pancakes. Mix together the blueberries, remaining sugar, and lime zest. Begin by placing 1 pancake on a plate, spoon and spread the blueberry mixture over the top of the pancake, top with another pancake, and repeat. Continue until there are no remaining pancakes or blueberry mixture. Cut the "cake" into slices and serve.

BLUEBERRY PANCAKE CAKE. TRY
TO SAY THAT OVER AND OVER AGAIN.
THIS CAKE IS ALWAYS BEST
WHEN EATEN RIGHT AFTER IT'S MADE.

ZABAGLIONE

6 servings

6 large egg yolks

½ cup (4 oz/125 g) sugar

½ cup (4 oz/125 ml) Marsala wine

¼ teaspoon salt

Whisk the egg yolks and sugar in a glass bowl set over a pan of boiling water. Use a hand mixer to blend the mixture until it is thick and golden in color, 4-6 minutes. Add the wine and salt and blend until all the ingredients are well integrated. Continue mixing until the sauce is thick and creamy in texture. Serve the sauce warm over fresh fruit.

THIS TRADITIONAL EGG-AND-SUGAR DESSERT IS DELICIOUS SERVED WITH FRESH BERRIES OR POURED OVER VANILLA CAKE.

STRAWBERRY & YOGURT SOUP

4 servings

2 pints (16 oz/500 g) strawberries, cleaned (a few sliced pieces reserved)

1¼ cups (10 fl oz/310 ml) fresh orange juice

1 cup (8 oz/250 g) vanilla yogurt

Combine the strawberries, orange juice, and yogurt in a blender and purée into a smooth soup consistency. Serve the soup chilled with a garnish of fresh strawberry slices.

THIS IS A SUPER EASY DESSERT SOUP. FOR AN ELEGANT TOUCH, SERVE IT IN A GLASS.

LIME−MARINATED MELON

4 servings

½ cup (4 oz/125 g) sugar

zest from 1 lime, finely chopped

juice from 1 lime

1 honeydew melon or cantaloupe, skin removed and sliced into thin halves

Combine ½ cup (4 fl oz/125 ml) water, the sugar, lime zest, and lime juice in a pot and bring the mixture to a boil. Cook the mixture until the sugar has dissolved. Divide the melon slices between 4 plates and pour the syrup over the top of each serving. Leave the melon at room temperature for 30 minutes before serving.

SERVING IDEA

This dish is excellent with slices of prosciutto served on the side.

> THIS IS A REALLY REFRESHING DISH
> THAT CAN BE SERVED AS
> AN APPETIZER OR DESSERT.

ICE CREAM SANDWICHES

4 servings

8 round, thin, sweet butter biscuits or cookies

4 scoops vanilla ice cream

honey, for drizzling

Place a scoop of ice cream between two biscuits, drizzle some honey on the ice cream, and serve.

VARIATIONS

Try serving this dish with caramel sauce and chocolate ice cream, or sliced strawberries and vanilla ice cream, or chocolate sauce and vanilla ice cream.

A SIMPLE, DELICIOUS DESSERT.

PAUL'S CARROT CAKE

10–12 servings

CAKE

½ cup (3½ oz/105 g) brown sugar, firmly packed

¾ cup (6 fl oz/180 ml) canola oil

4 large eggs

1¾ cups (7 oz/220 g) cake flour

1 teaspoon vanilla sugar

1 teaspoon baking powder

¼ teaspoon salt

1 teaspoon ground cinnamon

¾ lb (12 oz/375 g) carrots, grated

1 cup (6 oz/185 g) raisins

½ cup (2 oz/65 g) walnuts, chopped butter, for greasing

ICING

¾ cup (6 oz/165 g) cream cheese

8 tablespoons (4 oz/125 g) butter

2 cups (8 oz/250 g) confectioners' sugar

Preheat the oven to 350°F (180°C). Mix the brown sugar and oil together in a large bowl until you reach a smooth consistency. Add the eggs and stir well. Add the remaining ingredients for the cake and stir to an even consistency. Grease the insides of 2 bread pans with butter and divide the batter between the pans. Bake the cake until it is firm, about 50 minutes. A toothpick inserted in the center of the cake will come out clean when the cake is done. Set the cakes on a rack to cool. Stir together all the ingredients for the icing in a bowl and spread the icing over the top of the cakes.

> THIS CAKE HAS FOLLOWED ME THROUGH ALL MY YEARS. IT'S ALWAYS GOOD, WHETHER IT'S PRESENTED AS ONE LARGE CAKE OR IN TWO BREAD PANS.

RASPBERRY & ALMOND CAKE

8 servings

⅔ cup (5 oz/155 g) butter, softened

1 cup (7 oz/220 g) brown sugar, firmly packed

2 large eggs

1½ cups (6 oz/185 g) cake flour

¼ teaspoon salt

1 teaspoon baking powder

1 teaspoon vanilla sugar

1 cup (4½ oz/140 g) slivered almonds, toasted

1 pint (8 oz/250 g) fresh raspberries

Preheat the oven to 350°F (180°C). Stir the butter and brown sugar to an airy consistency. Stir in the eggs, one at a time. Add the flour, salt, baking powder, and vanilla sugar to the mixture and stir to a smooth consistency. Pour the mixture into a well-greased 9½-inch (24-cm) pan. Sprinkle the almonds and raspberries evenly over the top of the cake. Bake the cake until it is firm, about 50 minutes. Transfer the cake to a rack to cool, then cut into squares and serve at room temperature.

COOKING TIP

To toast the almond slivers, roast them in a hot oven until they brown evenly in color. When roasting nuts, the oils are released for flavor enhancement and they have a nicer texture. All nuts are good roasted before they're baked.

THE BASE OF THIS DESSERT IS DROP-DEAD DELICIOUS. IT HAS JUST ENOUGH CHOCOLATE IN IT, BUT NOT TOO MUCH.

RHUBARB & STRAWBERRY TART WITH CHOCOLATE

8 servings

¾ cup (12 tablespoons/6 oz/185 g) butter, softened

¼ cup (2 oz/50 g) sugar

2 large egg yolks

2 cups (8 oz/250 g) cake flour

¼ cup (¾ oz/20 g) cocoa powder

3 rhubarb stalks, cut into bite-sized pieces

⅓ cup (3 oz/90 g) sugar

1 pint (8 oz/250 g) fresh strawberries, cleaned and halved

fresh mint leaves, for garnish

whipped cream or ice cream, for serving

Start with the crust. Stir the butter, sugar, and egg yolks into a smooth consistency. Work the flour and cocoa powder into the mixture and stir vigorously. Knead the dough, transfer it to a bowl, cover it with plastic wrap, and refrigerate for 1 hour prior to use. Remove the dough from the refrigerator, roll it out, and press it into a greased pie pan. Prick the base of the dough with a fork over the entire surface. In a preheated 400°F (200°C) oven, bake the shell for about 15 minutes, or until the crust turns golden brown and crispy in texture. Transfer the crust to a rack to cool. Place the rhubarb and sugar in a nonstick pan and cook over medium heat. Cook until the rhubarb just begins to fall apart. Add the strawberries to the pan and stir. Spoon the contents of the pan into the pre-baked crust. Serve with whipped cream or ice cream and garnish with mint leaves.

INDEX

THANK YOU

Thanks to Cecelie Larvåg, who loaned her cottage with its beautiful surroundings, for her generosity. Thanks to Ingvild Flesland and Olaf Radermacher for letting us photograph in their beautiful home. Thanks to Sunniva Rademacher, Ana Dreyer Hensley, and Hanne Buxrud for their great help and assistance. Thanks to Christine Herra. And a huge thanks to Lars Røtterud, who allowed us to make Summer Food.